FLINTS
AND
FLASHES

NICHOLAS TRESILIAN

VOLUME THREE

✣

© Nicholas Tresilian 2023.
All rights reserved.

For two women who have brought me
so much happiness

Fay Tresilian

who died in 2009, just before our 40th wedding anniversary

and

Joanna Foster CBE

whom I first met Scottish dancing at the age of seventeen
and who agreed to marry me in 2015

❖

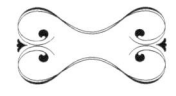

ACKNOWLEDGMENTS

This third sequence of random reminiscences and recollections was also, like the first and second, inspired by the fond memory of the Edwardian poet, E. H. Visiak (1878 – 1972) – author of, amongst his many titles, a short volume of poems, *Flints and Flashes*, published in Nonesuch Press in 1911. I have once again, in his honour, recycled the title of Visiak's slim volume - in its own way so appropriate for my own very different scattered thoughts and experiences.

My very grateful thanks also go to all those who directly inspired the creation of this book and contributed their energy, enterprise and scholarship to it:

My adored and adoring children, Arabella, Susannah and Alexander

My amanuensis extraordinaire, Jo Charrington

The graphic artist who gave form to this book, Graham Saunders

The proofreader who took such care with the final text, Jo Mortimer

And the rest of my wonderful family, for their abiding enthusiasm for this project, for their continuing inspiration and support, and for the joy they have given to my life: Sunnie, Mabel, Dorothy, Sienna, Samantha, George, Eleanor, Rosie, Ana-Sofía, Lucía, Mike, Nikki, Nouman, Kate, Annabel, Hugo, Sophie, Marcus, Thelma and Crispin

And to my beloved wife, Joanna Foster, for supporting this entire project whole-heartedly throughout

CONTENTS

Preface	IX
Falling ill	1
Royals at Lambrook	1
'A firebug is suspected'	3
Lost on Plynlimon	3
Prefect Flamingos	4
Princess Diana's gaze	5
Prince Charles's eyes	5
The immolation of the works of Oliver Jelly	6
The leper village outside Badminton	7
White hot technology	7
Mourning Mac Fisheries	8
Crudités	8
How to greet a gorilla	9
Jacaranda trees in Andalucia	9
Léger in Stuttgart	10
Chilean Margaux?	10
Newport versus Ravenna	10
Shrines in the Atacama Desert	11
The little knife grinder and the dinner in the hedge	12
Making a mule in West Virginia	13
Flying into Innsbruck	14
The American couple who had clocks instead of children	14
Ice Age animals on Weston-Super-Mare beach	15
Paul Hamlyn and the pursuit of silence	15
Getting lost in the Savile Club	16
London is a forest	17
BBC Armourers	17
Inspiring Claes Oldenburg	18
A meeting with Henry Moore	19

Tea with Mr and Mrs Moore	19
The meanness of the Brits	20
Widden Hill House heliograph	21
Lower Woods, Hawkesbury	21
Teddy Boys	22
Naked as Nature Intended	22
Such a disappointment...	23
They shall not pass!	23
Hobart's Funnies	24
The Virtues of Physical Gold	25
The day when Dwin Bramall sent me back	25
Constantin and Vaneta's marriages	26
A Bulgarian sales demonstration	27
John Julius Norwich and the sleeping policemen	28
The Powell's bull mastiff	29
Glass ashtray	30
Beating the retreat in Tripoli souk	31
Landing at Nice on my flight to Tripoli	32
Victory Days	33
Anthony Burgess at the Café Royal	34
William Gear	35
Moldovan who brought milk to Manhattan	36
Room 303	37
Early morning on Malaga beach	38
Picasso museum in Malaga	38
The drive along Blue Ridge Mountains	39
The English master and *Gray's Elegy*	*41*
Parking on ice beside a church in Canada	42
Mushroom soup in Poland	42
There but for the grace...	43
Chelsea Nick	43
Sir Henry Parker Bowles	44
A romantic tale	45

Vivat Imperium	45
Tenor who sang flat	46
Eheu! BBC Television Centre	47
The lonely donkey on the Beaufort estate	48
Jack Bishop	48
A helicopter assault	49
Thrown out of the hotel	50
Corin Redgrave's calfskin trousers	51
Three of clubs	53
You've never had it so good	53
A lump in my throat	54
Ladies' Night in Oldham	54
A question to the Oracle	54
Jane Russell	56
The Roman Centurion	57
Breakfast with the babushkas in St Petersburg	58
Betrayed by a bottle of rum	58
Buying Lypsyl in Bulgaria	59
My father and bananas	60
Clearing the beds from Netley Hospital after Suez	60
David Niven as an army officer	61
Kyiv and Lviv	61
A Flash of American Genius	62
Fleets flying home	67
Cesare the cat	67

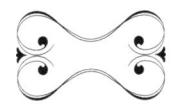

PREFACE

The important thing is to remain cheerful. I have been extraordinarily lucky. Writing *Flints and Flashes* gives me plenty of opportunity to bear witness to the wild variety of life, and yet somehow, like a charmed cat, I always find reason to feel I've landed right side up.

Even the devastating experience of my beloved wife Fay dying, quite suddenly of a stroke, led - as she would have wanted - to something beautiful. Our family friend Joanna Foster had also just lost her husband, Jerome, and the two of us, as friends since childhood when we first met dancing the Eightsome Reel in a village hall in Bristol, naturally got together. I would visit her in her tall Oxford house overlooking the River Cherwell and Magdalen Tower, and she would come to my flat in Lansdown Place West in Bath, and also for visits out to Las Pinedas, where she had first stayed with Fay and myself several years before.

This happiness has lasted. Joanna and I decided to live together in Cumnor, one of the villages surrounding Oxford - a village whose name had ever haunted me since first reading Matthew Arnold's *The Scholar-Gipsy* with its rustic image:

> 'At some lone homestead in the Cumnor hills,
> Where at her open door the housewife darns...'

Not that much darning was ever done, but our collective cheerfulness in Cumnor never abated, and the open door never closed.

We tied the marital knot a few years later on a rainy February day at St. Hilda's College in Oxford, surrounded by our respective families. By great good fortune our families adore each other, so every family gathering is a moment of great happiness, and mutual support at times of crisis is rapidly and effectively given.

We did not own the Cumnor house and it was by Joanna's genius that we spotted for sale the ground floor apartment of a beautiful mediaeval barn in old Kidlington, on a grey stone and much-flowered street leading directly to the village's famous church of St Mary. Somehow we managed to beat Covid and move house from Cumnor to Kidlington while the nation was mainly in lockdown.

To keep ourselves clear of Covid during the move, we hired a camper van which our vicar, Felicity Scroggie, invited us to park on her drive for the duration. Joanna was then in a position to work with our wonderful friend and help, Vivi Speck, at directing the placement of the furniture in the house - a bit here to the left - a bit here to the right, and so on. We also began the serious job of installing our extensive collection of works of art, starting with my dear friend Noel White's tremendous cave-painted door on our bedroom wall. The courtyard around the apartment was large enough to build an outside office for my work and my library. We had it painted a brilliant marine blue and surrounded it with big Spanish pots overflowing with flowers. On sunlit days its beach-hut blue positively lifts the heart.

We also had the great good fortune in Kidlington of meeting old friends and finding ourselves in a street where everyone seemed friendly. Soon after we arrived, an elderly Oxford professor, and world expert on the poems of Tennyson, volunteered to play Mozart on the piano in his sitting room, if the village were happy to gather around his open window. All this was part of the celebration of the NHS and the recognition of its triumph and courage during the Covid pandemic. How much I now owe the NHS for the wonderful treatment I have received.

All this gained greater meaning when, in 2021, I received a life-changing diagnosis: cancer of the lung. I have had the considerable fortune to feel the love and care of my adored Joanna, our families, our friends and neighbours, supporting me and us during these last few years. Conversations, poetry evenings and being read to have given me great joy. Having the strength to be able to dictate another volume of *Flints and Flashes* has been another source of delight. My thanks to all who have contributed.

We are extraordinarily happy here. Despite my dire diagnosis and the gloomy newscape both domestically and abroad, it is veritably impossible not to remain positive. Whence this third volume of my global reminiscences.

⁘

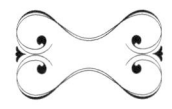

FALLING ILL

First it came in the form of water on the lung, accompanied by a bit of coughing. Then it came as cancer on the lung which the doctors said was too scattered to capture with radiotherapy. But with chemo they were going to hold it at bay. And so far so they have. Chemo is kindly administered but not much fun: it tends to knock you out for whole days on end. After two or three months of strong chemo I was transferred to a weaker maintenance chemo. The knockouts are still there but not so severe. I always dress up smartly when visiting the oncologist. I talk about writing and publishing books and generally give strong signs that I am participating strongly in life with the support of my beloved Joanna. I want them to continue believing that it is worth investing their drugs in me for as long as possible. And so on we go.

※

ROYALS AT LAMBROOK

I was touched to learn that the children of the Duke and Duchess of Cambridge had been assigned to Lambrook as their preparatory school. It has clearly gone upmarket since my day: the fees now are truly stupendous and Tesla cars are numerous on the driveway. But it was and is a very good school. The 18-

hole golf course was built in my day by the good Mr Ashworth, one of a temporary triplicate of three headmasters, himself more interested in golf than anything else during his short duration as a head. But the golf course – which I am glad to hear is still functioning some seventy-five years after I enjoyed dreamy rounds at dusk with my Mother's Mashie Niblick – stands as a real monument to the old enthusiast. It was also a school much given to adventures. It owned a wood, filled with bracken and tall shrubs with dark insides, but devoid of the brambles that rip the skin in so many wooded areas of Britain. When Boy Scouts were not building bridges or lighting fires to boil their Billy cans, much of their allocated time was spent in this magical playground of a wood, ending inevitably in the chasing game of 'French and English'.

The greatest adventure of my time was to celebrate the marriage of Princess Elizabeth and the Duke of Edinburgh. The whole school was turned into an armed stockade, and half the boys were assigned to defend it with chalk bombs – grenades made of chalkdust tightly wrapped in muslin which left a cloud through the air when thrown and an indelible white mark on the pullover of any boys successfully targeted. The other half of the school were assigned as the attackers and distributed around the local countryside to make their way into the grounds in various disguises – on the backs of tractors, in a wedding hearse and so on. I was one of the group located in the various big drawers of the local fire engine, which drove into the school – where we invaders were quickly unhoused and captured. The firemen then unfolded the main hose, and by a subtle connection with the school mains, managed to produce a magnificently curving stream of celebratory water. Tea and cakes followed. It was a perfect day. Classes resumed the following morning.

Since my time, Lambrook has extended to include girls and is very much bigger than the one hundred total boys with whom I learned and played in the 1940s and '50s. According to the press, it still lies open to all kinds of adventure.

'A FIREBUG IS SUSPECTED'

The newsroom at Southern Television contained a wide range of characters amongst its sub-editors and secretaries. One sub in particular appeared to specialise in arson stories. Whenever a barn burned down in East Grinstead or a yacht was set fire to in a marina, he would end his report: 'a firebug is suspected'. The belief amongst his colleagues in those far off days was that he himself must have been an amateur arsonist.

LOST ON PLYNLIMON

I once took my ten-year-old son Alexander to West Wales with the purpose of climbing that poetically named mountain Plynlimon. We stayed in a very comfortable hotel, Gliffaes Country House Hotel in Crickhowell, now alas extinct, and the next morning set out, well equipped with climbing boots and Mackintoshes – those were the days – to stride up the mountain, which was easily conceivable at our respective ages. It was a rough day with low cloud and a bouncing wind. We were three-quarters of the way up the mountain when the cloud settled around us, and we were suddenly completely lost in a grey haze of conflicting directions. Attempting to return to the base of the mountain proved unsuccessful in those deeply beguiling mists. We remained lost on Plynlimon till the cloud lifted and we could finally scramble to the peak before making our way down to the security of the car park at the foot of the mountain. It was a lesson in how easy it is to be overwhelmed and even quite scared by the natural chaos of mists and fogs. The problem with chaos in any dimension, whether geographical or political, is that all natural points of direction disappear.

⁘

PREFECT FLAMINGOS

There was a lake near our house in Spain which was home to tens of thousands of pink flamingos. Every morning at dawn, a vast cloud of flamingos would rise up, fly the fifty or so kilometres to Doñana National Park, fill up their bills by feeding in the worm rich marshes, fly back to their home lake and disgorge their beaks to their respective children. Remarkably, not all the adults took part in this daily migration. A small cohort of – one assumes – elderly birds were left behind on the original lake to protect and organise the children of the adults on their arduous flights to and from Doñana – elderly males and females temporarily assuming the role of prefect at a British boarding school.

⁘

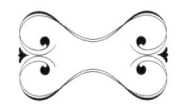

Royal Eyes

PRINCESS DIANA'S GAZE

Once, at a Mansion House dinner, I momentarily intercepted the gaze of Princess Diana scanning the room from the top table. Her eyes were so startlingly bright and commanding, being caught in her gaze was quite like being shot.

⁜

PRINCE CHARLES'S EYES

At a Classic FM concert at the Banqueting Hall at Whitehall, I had the pleasure of being introduced to the then Prince of Wales. I explained I was chairman of a local radio station – Wiltshire Radio as it was then known – which served his country house at Highgrove. He dipped into his pockets and gave me a card, naming the Head of the Prince of Wales's Trust. Much later, I managed to persuade Classic FM to perform a concert in Hyde Park to raise money for the Trust. I still remember the energy of his expression and the warmth of his eyes.

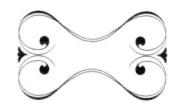

THE IMMOLATION OF THE WORKS OF OLIVER JELLY

Oliver Jelly was a distinguished Midlands surgeon with a special knowledge of the intricacies of the golf swing – on which he had published a book and was an acknowledged expert. However, he was also a very talented printmaker, and the time in his life came when he decided to retire from surgery and dedicate his life solely to making prints. To this end, he bought a windmill tower in Cardiganshire as a home and an abandoned motor garage – complete with inspection pit – to function as his studio. He was a friend of Arthur Giardelli and often came to visit when I was there. He always wore an immaculately tailored hunt coat and corduroy trousers. I have one of his prints. It is of a combine harvester crossing a cornfield. It is calm and canonically simple: it took an Oliver Jelly to make a work of art out of a combine harvester. But alas one day, while in full creative flow at the abandoned garage, Oliver stepped backwards into the inspection pit, broke his neck and died. His family came down from the Midlands – they don't think too much of artists there – and executed their opinions by burning his entire remaining work.

THE LEPER VILLAGE OUTSIDE BADMINTON

Every year Badminton House in Gloucestershire holds its world-famous three-day event for riders of up to Olympic standard. Few, if any, amongst the thousands of visitors to the great annual event with its three days of Dressage, Cross-Country and Show Jumping would have had the means to guess that the distant pile of stones beyond the Cross-Country course in the furthest reaches of the Badminton estate was once a hamlet built exclusively for lepers to keep them away from Badminton village, with its thriving population of healthy peasants and finely mounted grandees. The stones stand there as a silent testimony to the terror that leprosy struck in the souls of men and women in mediaeval England – an age of many other fatal plagues also. It is certainly not the only village of its kind. To the enquiring eye, the British countryside betrays many such wretched but quasi-charitable institutions.

⁂

WHITE HOT TECHNOLOGY

Brian Trubshaw, the original test pilot of Concorde, who was one night a dinner guest of my old friend and Bristol Aerospace pilot Tregarron Griffiths, told the story of the first flight on Concorde by Anthony Wedgwood Benn (aka Tony Benn), then Minister of Technology, which he himself in the Bond mood of the time christened 'Mintech'. Benn had actually opposed the development of Concorde from his seat in Parliament, but nonetheless was thrilled to be the first British minister to take a ride on this magnificent product of English and French imagination.

The plane took off. After a while, the engines cut out, Trubshaw pressed the button for the reserve system, and the plane began to function normally again. Benn was not informed. Nor was he informed when, yet again, the first reserve system cut out and Trubshaw pressed the button for the second reserve system. There was no third reserve system so, completely unprotected, Concorde was banked round and hastily returned to *terra firma* at Filton. The Minister drove away full of pride in this wonderful engineering project.

⁜

MOURNING MAC FISHERIES

I do miss the days when every high street included an open front and a great marble slab angled towards the street and displaying a fine array of fresh fishes for cats and/or humans.

⁜

CRUDITÉS

At the time when my Aunt Kitty died in her late eighties, she was still employing a German au pair. I asked the German au pair to stay on and house-sit, protecting my aunt's valuables until they went for sale. Kitty had one very fine Georgian coffee pot. The German au pair's boyfriend stole it – I forget how I discovered. I went down to Brighton to interview the au pair. If I threw her out, the whole house would be exposed to visiting cat burglars. I took the au pair out to dinner at a local, rather upmarket restaurant above Marine Parade. I told her

I had decided to trust her, and I wished her to stay on in the house until the clearers came. I have always remembered that dinner because of its first course which featured crudités – the French word for chopped raw vegetables and fruit. The crudités worked. The au pair – whose name I cannot now recall – stayed for the required period, protected the house, and stole nothing. But then crudités signify a certain honesty and candour. On this occasion, their symbolism was not wasted.

❖

HOW TO GREET A GORILLA

How would you behave were you, while sauntering through Kensington Gardens, suddenly to meet a gorilla? According to Professor Nick Humphrey of Darwin College, Cambridge, who studied gorillas in the jungle with the celebrated Dian Fossey, the routine for greeting is the following. First, slap your chest loudly. Then go to the nearest shrub or leafy tree, break off branches and make a nest of them, then sit in it confidently.

What the wardens of Kensington Gardens would have to say about that, I leave to the reader's imagination.

❖

JACARANDA TREES IN ANDALUCIA

Spring is the season for Jacaranda trees, with their purple clouds of blossom lining the streets of the big cities of southern Spain.

LÉGER IN STUTTGART

In the course of my intercontinental business, I once engaged a lawyer in Stuttgart who was recommended by a good friend. But on the wall before which I sat was a large painting by Fernand Léger worth many millions of euros. Given the limited fee-paying abilities of my ambitious but rather small English independent radio group, I looked at the Léger, I looked at the lawyer and then, in the best traditions of British journalism, I made my excuses and left.

⁜

CHILEAN MARGAUX?

From my experience of travel in Chile, the very best red wine available was brazenly labelled after the great French classic Margaux. It remains a mystery what the *vignerons* of Bordeaux – home of the original *appellation controlée* Margaux – have to say about that.

⁜

NEWPORT VERSUS RAVENNA

With my wife Fay and our three children, I had driven to Newport for the opening of an exhibition by the great Welsh artist Ivor Davies. On driving into the underground car park below the art gallery, I managed to mistake the Lord Chief Justice of Wales as a parking attendant – a misidentification which he accepted with some grace. We walked out into the street to access the gallery.

There was that strange atmosphere in the air, characteristic of cities where the young are gathering for a Friday night's fight but are still just gathering into groups, ready for the tribal conflict to come. When we re-emerged from the exhibition, the fight was on. There were boys yelling obscenities. There were boys urinating in shop doorways. There were presumably more numerate boys urinating into the letterboxes of banks, which in those days were there mainly to accept and make secure the daily bank deposits of small traders. Other boys were playing loud football with beer cans. My children's eyes were out on stalks at this wild pattern of behaviour compared with their usual rural life. It was impossible not to note that all the noisy young thugs were boys.

Two days later, Fay and I arrived at Venice airport and took a water taxi to the main station beside the Grand Canal. Three hours later, we were in our hotel in Ravenna, where we had gone to see the Byzantine mosaics. Below us, the square was full of young couples circulating on their evening *passeggiata*, murmuring peaceably to each other. At the head of the square was a motorbike shop, but no heavy metal crowd around it. All was peaceful and civilised. I wished my children had been there to witness it.

⁘

SHRINES IN THE ATACAMA DESERT

A great main road joins Chile with its neighbouring Peru. Heavy lorries thunder along it every day, and not all of them arrive safely. As the highway crosses the limitless monotony of the Atacama Desert, the desire to sleep seems to overcome many drivers. All along the grand highway – and the winding roads which join it from the Andes – are shrines to drivers who fell asleep and died in their cabs. Several use the whole cab of the vehicle as a memorial. Often, there are several small chairs for mourners to sit round the grave – also empty bottles for pouring libations. The ancient American belief systems still live on in Chile.

Once, on the way back to our Rancho-style hotel in the middle of the desert, we came across a particularly elaborate arrangement of concrete pillars and altar tables – a chapel of remembrance open to the burning wind and the stars. My wife, Fay, who had been photographing these curiously anonymous shrines, had unbuttoned her Leica and was probing the site with her lens when a large white bus drew up, and forty or more people poured out of it. The politics of Chile were still volatile: I advised Fay to put her camera away. But when the people crossed the road to us, they wanted to tell us about the terrible road crash that had occurred at that spot, killing many of their relatives. Reality comes back to life with surprising rapidity in the deserts of South America.

⁙

THE LITTLE KNIFE GRINDER AND THE DINNER IN THE HEDGE

Knife grinders in the UK seem long to have disappeared. But once upon a time – forty and more years ago – knife grinders still existed in backward areas like Wiltshire. A particular knife grinder with a rusty bike and a sparkling whetstone driven from the pedals when the bike was on its stand, used routinely to visit us in Luckington. One day, my ever-inquisitive daughter Arabella got into conversation with the knife grinder and discovered that, while his winter place of residence was in the stable block of Easton Grey House – a big manor house nearby – his preferred place of residence in summer was a hedgerow beside the road to Malmesbury. He invited us to come and have supper with him. A couple of days later, Arabella and I drove up the road towards Malmesbury, spotted a rusty bike leaning against a gap in the hedgerow, and there was our friend, boiling a large bone in an old saucepan on a fire amidst the roots of the blackthorn hedge. We were regally received and given glasses of the rich bone broth, scented with local roadside herbs. Squeezed into our friend's very private space, Arabella and I felt hugely honoured.

Alas, even knife grinders of the most singular robustness and the rustiest of bikes are mortal. We never saw our friend again and learned later that he had died. His rusty bike with its heavy flywheel was never seen again.

⁕

MAKING A MULE IN WEST VIRGINIA

My unit was filming in a farmyard in West Virginia (with vast amounts of uranium rock underground – a characteristic of the wealth of the area). It was an empty farmyard – no live animals. I suggested it would be more atmospheric, and therefore more suitable for filming, if there was, for instance, a mule available. 'Whazza mule?' I explained that a mule was a hybrid of a male donkey and a female horse. We returned to our work. Half an hour later, an immense low loader appeared in the farmyard. In it was a jackass and a broodmare. It was a wonderful example of American generosity, but at that moment I was travelling around the world for Reuters and could not interrupt my journey for the 343 days of the gestation period required for the amorous couple in the low loader to produce an actual mule. Like the reporter in the *News Chronicle*, we made our excuses and left.

FLYING INTO INNSBRUCK

Flying into Innsbruck is a slightly scary thing. One's aeroplane has to fly between great walls of rock on either side with a narrow margin between wingtip and cliff face. It is enough to make any passenger nervous. But Austrian Airlines have evolved a method for calming their passengers down. Two sublimely beautiful air hostesses strap themselves into seats facing the passengers, at least reassuring the anxious male that should the plane hit a rock, there would be a direct route to paradise.

✥

THE AMERICAN COUPLE WHO HAD CLOCKS INSTEAD OF CHILDREN

America is a land of infinite surprises. I was once led to knock on a front door in South Carolina. The door opened, the owner of the house appeared, but his greeting to us was almost drowned out by a carillon of clock chimes, each one counting the hour. The house owner and his wife had chosen to have clocks instead of children and had furnished their house with dozens of fine old clocks – a multitude of different shapes and sizes. Our host's wife assured us that if a single clock chimed out of time, even in the great cloud of sound that arose every hour, like a baby crying for milk, they could always identify its sound and go to put the unhappy clock right.

✥

ICE AGE ANIMALS ON WESTON-SUPER-MARE BEACH

Fields behind Weston-super-Mare are the home territory of one of Britain's least known institutions: The British Spotted Pony Society[1]. Spotted horses are officially identified by the patterns of spots across the body, the area of mottled skin around the eyes and striped hooves – a combination which sharply distinguishes them from the piebald and skewbald ponies familiar at children's gymkhanas. The ponies appear on Weston-super-Mare beach and seem to represent an ancient strand of Gypsy culture. The ponies carry thousands of children on their backs every year and, despite their Neolithic origins, are extremely well behaved.

❖

PAUL HAMLYN AND THE PURSUIT OF SILENCE

Wiltshire Radio, in its determination to speak for the region it represented and not be overwhelmed by heavy external interests, had limited shareholders to a maximum investment. One potential investor, however, geographically resident in the region, wanted to raise his stake to some ten times the stated maximum. He was Paul Hamlyn (1926 - 2001), the millionaire founder of the immensely popular series Music for Pleasure, and many other enterprises. He lived in a magnificent Jacobean manor in the Cotswolds with a vast French fireplace in the drawing-room. We drank an introductory glass of champagne in front of the giant fireplace, and I was then bidden to the publisher's office: an intimate room in the rear of the house. There, Hamlyn sat down and, without further speech,

---

[1] The British Spotted Pony Society evolved when the horse and pony elements of the British Spotted Horse & Pony Society went their separate ways in 1977.

looked at me. 'Aha,' I surmised, 'One of those: the strong man who unnerves and dominates whoever he is addressing by masterfully withholding his speech.' I recognised the type of negotiator – and to a degree understood his position. Hamlyn was an immensely generous man in the provision of money for good causes, and we were asking him to reduce rather than increase his holding – almost certainly not an experience he was accustomed to. These thoughts went through my head as we both sat in silence as I was not going to be the one to speak first. Our silent interview, like the dialogue of two Roman statues on a beach, was finally broken open by the arrival of my Finance Director, Henry Meakin. A compromise was arranged in the form of a reduced shareholding, but as a Director on the Board. We never heard from Hamlyn again.

⁘

GETTING LOST IN THE SAVILE CLUB

The Savile Club is one of Mayfair's most charming gentlemen's clubs. But God defend any stranger who is summoned by a call of nature to the warren of corridors beneath the club. I once found myself wandering this warren for a full fifteen minutes before another human being appeared and showed me the way upstairs. A chastened Orpheus, I made my way back to the dining room where my absent-minded host had barely even noticed my long disappearance. I have no idea whether the man who showed me the escape route from the cellars was not trapped like Eurydice in that gentlemen's Hades forever.

⁘

LONDON IS A FOREST

Back in the days before the BBC evacuated its Television Centre in White City, I once climbed up the East Tower – dedicated *inter alia* to the BBC Documentaries department – and also including the Armourers for when it was necessary to pick up a pistol. Arriving at the very top of the building, I stepped out on the balcony and was astonished: London is not so much a city as a forest. Thousands of terraced houses stretched away into the distance, all of them with trees in their gardens, often smothering a view of the house itself. This was in the days before the experience of green nature was considered essential to health, but it was a marvellously cheering sight – a quite new way of understanding London.

⁂

BBC ARMOURERS

I only once in my life visited the BBC Armourers, in 1965. It was to pick up a suitably disarmed Webley pistol – the type with which young British officers were all too frequently sent to their graves in armed combat – a deeply inaccurate weapon with an awful kick. However, on this occasion the pistol was completely disarmed, and I packed it into a pocket and left. I needed the pistol for some kind of spoof I had written for *Late Night Line Up*. The story involved the theft of George Brown's National Plan for the British Economy. I found the Plan micro-dotted as a beauty spot on the cheek of one of the models in the window of the Mary Quant shop. The exciting moment of the story, however, involved my emerging, pistol in hand, from St James's Park tube station and marching fearlessly towards the opposite building, which happened to be New Scotland Yard.

In those far-off pacific days, the sight of a young man in a suit advancing on the police headquarters with a pistol seemed to arouse no interest at all – nowadays, one would probably be shot dead first and questioned afterwards.

⁙

INSPIRING CLAES OLDENBURG

I was with Claes Oldenburg, one of the leading pioneers in Pop Art, on a visit to E.J. Power[2], the well-known collector of Modern Art. Oldenburg noticed the peculiar way in which I stubbed out my cigarettes by bending over the filter to crush out the burning tobacco in the lit end – resulting in a squashed 'L' shape. Before he left, Oldenburg obtained a small tin and scooped my strangely shaped cigarette into it, for transport back to the USA. Shortly afterwards, Oldenburg produced a number of giant cigarette sculptures based on my 'design'. It is the only time I have consciously been involved with inspiring a piece of contemporary art.

Claes Oldenburg (b. 1929), Giant Fagends, 1967

---

2   E.J. (or Ted) Power (1899-1993) was the first, and for a period, the only substantial collector of contemporary art in Britain.

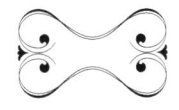

Henry Moore

A MEETING WITH HENRY MOORE

The day before I visited Henry Moore, I had been at the Tate gallery studying Sargent's image of Ruskin fording the boulders of a mountain stream. Arriving at Much Hadham a day later, I was led by one of Moore's apprentices through an entire estate of small greenhouses full of sticks, stones and bones awaiting conversion into matrices for Moore's future sculptures. When I arrived in Moore's drawing room, my eyes were immediately engaged by a fine picture of a woodland stream. "Is that a Sargent?" I asked Moore. "No," he replied. "It's a Cezanne." A work of art infinitely more valuable.

✥

TEA WITH MR AND MRS MOORE

Our interview was interrupted by tea, which was served on a long shiny mahogany table on fine china. Apprentices were on either side, with Mr and Mrs Moore at the head and tail, respectively. I realised then that this great modern Master had created for himself the perfect replica of a classical artist's atelier.

THE MEANNESS OF THE BRITS

As I left, Moore murmured to me that though his sculptures were located around the world, the British had been disappointingly slow in buying any of them.

❖

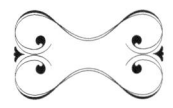

WIDDEN HILL HOUSE HELIOGRAPH

Widden Hill House on the very brim of the Cotswolds overlooking the River Severn and the Black Mountains beyond was where I spent much of my teenage years. It had been the Vicarage for the village of Horton in Gloucestershire. However, it was perched on the very rim of the Cotswolds: a long and tiring scramble from the church itself. This was because the vicar who built it sometime in the early 19th century had a brother in the Black Mountains on the far side of the River Severn. Both brothers had heliographs and used these products of early science to communicate across the fifty or so miles that separated their two houses.

⁜

LOWER WOODS, HAWKESBURY

Lower Woods was a scrambling forest at the very foot of the Cotswolds. In summer, my father used to drive out there to listen to nightingales. But the most sensational event at Lower Woods occurred when the two local hunts, the Beaufort and the Berkeley, chose to draw the woods for foxes on the same Saturday morning. History does not record the amount of miscegenation which occurred on that happy day for hounds, but disentangling the two packs took the entire morning and few foxes were seriously pursued that day – I think of this as the day of the apoplectic whippers-in.

TEDDY BOYS

The West of England was always a bit behind the times. Teddy Boys came relatively late to the region, and they were not particularly nice. They wore a peacock costume of long hair, flashy suits known as 'drapes', and rubber soled shoes, known as 'brothel creepers'. Their favourite weapon was the bicycle chain.

The Teddy Boys booked themselves a regular night every week in the pub at Iron Acton, where we lived at that time. Their end came, however, when they decided to start a fight at the village fete at nearby Hawkesbury Upton. Hawkesbury was largely populated by the descendants of Irish labourers imported to dig the railway tunnel, which carries the Great Western Railway from England into Wales. Its inhabitants were legendarily tough. There was a particular area of council housing known to the locals as 'Little Russia', where no one's prize vegetables growing for the village fete were safe. The Bristol Teddy Boys' visit, on the other hand, provided a different kind of distraction. Legend has it that they ended the afternoon lying in stunned rows in the village hall.

✥

NAKED AS NATURE INTENDED

When I was in my late teens, my sister Liz, leading a dashing social life at Bristol Art College, decided to modernise me. She took me to a cinema which specialised in nudist films. These films were intrinsically very chaste. A lot of handball was played, but invariably behind low shrubs, which provided a kind of modesty veil for the participants. However, this particular film – the name of which I can no longer recollect – contained that episode so attractive to writers of high opera including Mozart and Tchaikovsky: the letter writing scene. The stage set for the letter writing scene in this particular film was one of those 1950's dressing tables with three interconnected mirrors. The camera peeked over the shoulder of the girl writing the letter to take a view of the three mirrors. Thus, the viewer received the benefit of three bosoms for the price of one.

✥

SUCH A DISAPPOINTMENT...

It is the duty of every traveller to the state of Arizona to make a detour to see the Grand Canyon, a hugely impressive gash in the sandstone mountains made over many millennia by the Colorado River. It was not unusual for tourists of the tougher type to trek down to the bottom of the canyon and then trek panting up again. I was standing in one of the lookout posts on the very rim of the canyon when beside me, a middle-aged American said to his friend – with evident false regret, "My wife and I were planning to go down to the bottom of the canyon but she is ill, and I have to be home to look after her so I cannot go."

✥

THEY SHALL NOT PASS!

One of the great technological miracles of World War II was the Mulberry floating harbour of concrete caissons, drawn across the Channel by armoured tugs and then assembled into two separate harbours, one at Omaha Beach and the other at Arromanches. The Marines who came aboard at Arromanches unrolled long rubber mats so that tanks emerging from the landing craft should not get stuck in the sand. One of these long rubber mats ran straight up to a house facing the beach which effectively blocked its way. The house happened to belong to the Mayor of Arromanches. When the Marines explained to him that they would have to blow up his house to get their tanks through, he replied with dignity that it would be better if they blew up his immediate neighbour's house – and so they did. The gap where the mayor's neighbours once lived and through which the Marines drove their floating tanks still exists today.

After touring the site and marvelling at the model of the harbour in the museum, I found myself a restaurant and had a truly memorable *fruits de mer* while overlooking what is nowadays no longer a bloodstained scene.

✣

HOBART'S FUNNIES

The swimming tanks are one of the family of UK war machines developed especially for the invasion, based on variants of the Churchill tank and known collectively as 'Hobart's Funnies' after Major-General Percy Hobart, Commander of the 79th Armoured Division. Versions included a tank with a large net across its bow equipped to hold enough timber to tip into an enemy trench and make it passable. Others included a tank with an adapted Howitzer in its turret, designed to blow up enemy pillboxes. I write of these with particular affection because the father of my second wife, Joanna, Lieutenant Colonel Michael Meade was one of the team of British officers who developed these exotic vehicles and delivered them to the Normandy battlefields.

✣

THE VIRTUES OF PHYSICAL GOLD

I was standing in line to show my passport at Charles de Gaulle Airport, when the young Belgian banker in front of me in his immaculate Savile Row suit said to his neighbour in the queue: 'In three different wars, my family has found it useful to own gold'. The three wars were evidently the Franco-Prussian, followed by World Wars I and II. Having the coinage in hand meant having a ready means for bribing the *Gauleiter*.

❖

THE DAY WHEN DWIN BRAMALL SENT ME BACK

It was one of my first days on exercise in the Libyan desert. Dwin Bramall[3] – then my company commander – had sent me off on what was evidently some kind of test. I was to explore a deep wadi until I found some signs of human life. I set off up the riverbed between beetling cliffs hung with the coffins of the ruling Senussi class – rendered safe from brigands and desert foxes by the inaccessible positions of their ancient wooden coffins. The wadi itself – a dried up river – was full of immense boulders. I scrambled amongst these giants' marbles until thoroughly bored and exhausted. I found no human trace and decided to go back to report it. My company commander was unimpressed. He sent me back to go further. I scrambled grumpily along more riverbed, when suddenly arrested by the smell of wood smoke. A few moments later, I was looking across the wadi at a little paradise of isolated life. A round hut of branches from thorn bushes subtended a thorn hedge,

---

3 Field Marshal Edwin Noel Westby Bramall, Baron Bramall, KG, GCB, OBE, MC, JP, DL (1923 – 2019)

within which stood the owner of the farm and a couple of goats. Outside the hedge was a brilliant green lawn – possibly rye or wheat in its early stages of growth. The whole scene indicated the presence of a hidden well or spring giving plentiful water. My task accomplished, I stumbled back along the wadi and was readmitted to the fold by my company commander. The vision of that little totally self-sufficient farm remote from all visible form of communication still hovers vividly in my mind today.

❖

CONSTANTIN AND VANETA'S MARRIAGES

I was invited as a guest to the marriage of my colleague Constantin Tilev and Vaneta, a newsreader at *Radio FM Plus*. The first ceremony took place in the registry office. Unlike the sometimes chilly formality of an English registry office, the office in Sofia was an oasis of personal warmth and friendship – as such distinguishing itself from most of the chilly bureaucracy of life under Communism. After a ceremony noted for its smiles and laughter, the entire wedding party moved off to the nearest Orthodox church for the religious ceremony – which reaches its climax when crowns are rotated above the heads of bride and groom. During the course of the service, a modest crowd of children had accumulated outside the church gate. Their waiting was now rewarded with bags of boiled sweets and chocolate gaily flung over the church wall. Various vehicles now carried us up the slopes of Mount Vitosha to the hotel, destined for the wedding breakfast. Unlike a British marriage ceremony where bride and groom and associated relations form a line to greet a long queue of guests before obediently sitting down for lunch and speeches, in Bulgaria it is still customary for the newly married couple to consummate their betrothal in a literal way, by disappearing upstairs to a bedroom for a considerable period of time. Meanwhile, a white sheet had been laid down in the doorway to the dining room and a red scarf laid upon it – eliminating all doubt as to what might be going on. Finally, after time for several guests to fall asleep from the strong effects of Rakia, the happy couple appeared in the doorway, where they were greeted with a ritual gift of salt by Tilev's tiny mother. It has proved a very successful union, fruitful with children and marked by many signs of happiness.

⁂

A BULGARIAN SALES DEMONSTRATION

During my time on the board of *Radio FM Plus*, my principal concern had been to transfer the culture of British commercial radio – culture both in commercial terms and in programming – and thus turn *Radio FM Plus* into a station with a large and loyal listenership – a trick we subsequently sought to repeat with stations in the Black Sea ports of Varna and Burgas.

GWR numbered amongst its staff a sales training expert who was also a part-time member of the paratroopers. His name was Mike. I brought him out to Bulgaria to teach sales techniques to the sales team. The group spent a busy day's training at Borovets in the Rila Mountains, then took themselves out to dinner at a restaurant and finally repaired to their hotel for a convivial evening drink. Luckily, it turned out that Mike had military experience. He was first to recognise the crack and patter of machine pistols firing into the ceiling of the bar. He spun round, saw three men standing in the bar doorway with guns, and shouted to everyone to hit the ground. Fortunately, no one was hurt, though there was a prominent bullet hole in the back of the seat on which our Head of Sales had previously been sitting. The gunmen presently ceased firing at the ceiling and disappeared from the door. Our rather shaken sales force staggered to their feet, to observe that no bottles had been broken in the bar and no barmen had been hurt.

The entire scary episode was in fact a sales demonstration – Bulgarian style. Hotels in the Bulgarian skiing resort were 'protected' by so-called insurance companies. The manager of the current insurance company at our hotel had been sacked – and had decided immediately upon his revenge. He and his 'insurance' colleagues drove up to the hotel in big, black glazed BMWs with blue and white dice rattling in the windows, charged into the hotel, tied up the existing staff to prove how useless they were, did their trick with the machine pistols and drove away. We never knew whether the new company got the job, but everyone involved in it was known because of the peculiar conditions obtaining contracts in Bulgaria at that time.

✣

JOHN JULIUS NORWICH AND THE SLEEPING POLICEMEN

John Julius Norwich had invited a film industry friend, Nicholas Brabourne, to dinner in his cottage deep in the Wiltshire countryside. My wife, Fay, and I were also guests. The evening *inter alia* celebrated the fact that both Norwich and Brabourne had accompanied their fathers to the Nuremberg Trials of the leaders of the Nazi party, held immediately after the war. At one point, the conversation slipped away from high matters to the fact that John Julius' farmer landlord had fixed sleeping policemen in thick concrete at intervals along the full length of the long drive which gave access to John Julius's rural den. I coined the phrase *'les flics au bois dormant'*. John Julius, echoing Oscar Wilde, said "I wish I had said that..."

⁌

THE POWELL'S BULL MASTIFF

Tommy Powell was Chippenham's principal auctioneer. He and his wife Molly lived in an enchanting cottage full of 19th-century paintings of the best kind. We frequently entertained each other, usually at Sunday lunches. One Sunday lunchtime, there was a new character on the scene: a large bull mastiff. Given that the Powells' cottage was located in the rural countryside and contained many treasures, an impressive guard dog seemed quite a rational addition to the household. To my surprise, the dog and I got on tremendously well. All dogs like being tickled under the chin, and this great guard dog was as soppy as you could imagine. We had drinks and then lunch.

I remember Tommy talking about his time in the Wiltshire Regiment during the invasion of Normandy and of the point-blank accuracy of the twenty-five pounder guns of the British Royal Artillery. Tommy was lucky to survive as part of the 250,000 men who landed in Normandy under Montgomery. They resisted the German Panzers and turfed the German infantry out of the *bocage* – a grand army of brave civilians.

After lunch, we drank coffee, said our farewells and then walked down the drive with the Powells and their dog. Suddenly, I felt a ferocious clamp on my arm. The guardian dog had changed its mind: I was no longer a friend. I was an enemy. With much pleading, Tommy and Molly persuaded the dog to release me before Fay and I reached our car and drove away. There is something very strange about being bitten by your friend's guard dog. It seemed to create a psychological break on both sides. To my great regret, I never saw the Powells again.

✣

GLASS ASHTRAY

One of my closest supporters on the Wiltshire Radio board was Harold Cory, a publisher who had made himself fabulously wealthy by bidding successfully for a business park outside Salisbury. This enabled him to acquire a magnificent house in Salisbury's Cathedral Close, with a view of the cathedral spire and lawns going down to the legendary River Avon, in much the same way as Constable must have seen them. Harold – who once tried to persuade me to become a Liberal MP – became my vice-chairman and head of a sprawling collection of advisory groups which were part of our licence application offer.

Harold had somehow negotiated access to the mediaeval gate leading into the Close. His office, heavily ornamented with gothic pillars and pilasters, was in the room above. The Corys were near neighbours of Ted Heath, who lived a couple of Georgian frontages along the Close in Mompesson House. He was a regular visitor to the Corys' Christmas parties, where he took much pleasure in Harold's collection of Frank Brangwyn's paintings – Brangwyn in his day had been the ruling prince of the Royal Academy. But fashion fell away and who remembers him now?

One weekend, I was invited down to Salisbury for a picnic lunch in the Corys' Georgian gazebo beside the River Avon. The star guest that day was a well-known BBC news reporter from whom we learned that the best paid job in the BBC was Washington correspondent – generous in expenses and largely tax-free.

At the end of lunch, Harold's wife, Olga, took the tray and manoeuvred down the garden to take it into the kitchen. By this time, I too needed a comfort break and set off towards the house. As I crossed the hall to the downstairs loo, a cry came from the drawing-room: "I hate that man and all his snobby media friends." At the same moment, a heavy glass ashtray with rectangular edges, clearly hurled by Olga, exploded on the wall a yard in front of me. I found Olga in the drawing-room, wearing the slightly fazed expression of someone who has just thrown a potentially-lethal weapon against the wall. "Olga, you really mustn't do that," I said. "You nearly killed me." We walked together up the garden to the gazebo and nothing else was said – though I suppose a broken ashtray would have to be explained in some way later on.

⁙

BEATING THE RETREAT IN TRIPOLI SOUK

The nearest I ever came in Libya to being under fire was in the souk at Tripoli. At our previous base in Derna, it was normal for crowds of little boys to come up begging for *baksheesh* – spare cash from we apparently wealthy British officers. In Derna, it was customary to tell them to *imshi* – British army speak for f- off. They would obediently run away.

Tripoli was a different case. When the boys ran up demanding *baksheesh* – and there were three of us on this occasion, including one regular – we uttered the usual *imshi* and marched on, whereupon we came under a hail of old tin cans, bottles and the odd small stone. I remember the regular officer setting the lead by maintaining a smart military march through the souk until we were clear of attack. I noted that, as his two companions, we followed his example in maintaining military discipline while '*withdrawing to prepared positions*' – the army's famous phrase for abject retreat.

The same rigidly upright regular soldier later stepped out of the army and joined the Stock Exchange – in those days always welcome to members from the upper classes. Female relatives in his family were universally brilliant and most of them left books which have become classics of English literature. My colleague from the 60th Rifles was put in charge of a new computerised trading system at the Stock Exchange, but though he was of good birth, he was no mathematician, and the system rather spectacularly failed.

❖

LANDING AT NICE ON MY FLIGHT TO TRIPOLI

My first ever flight occurred when I had received my commission and was posted to the First Battalian 60th Rifles, at that time based in an old Italian army barracks in Derna, Libya. We took off from Blackbushe, a little-used airport even in those days, but a great target for owners of fast cars who would use the long single runway as an occasion to 'do the ton' – achieve 100mph. Now the time was near midnight and the racing cars had all gone home. The belief in those days was that it was safer to have the plane's seats facing backwards towards the tail. This gave the back of the chairs some support in case of a sudden crash landing. When I boarded, the 'safe' seats had been packed with riflemen. As for we three officers travelling with them, we were put in the technically much less safe seats at the back of the plane looking forward. It was an interesting illustration of military thinking: officers were always expected to give the lead by taking the most dangerous role!

I had a window for the flight and was completely captivated by the novel sight of tiny cars and vans buzzing through the French countryside five thousand feet below. We had departed in the dark but, as dawn rose over southern France, we landed to refuel and to change from heavy serge British battledress into the khaki drill uniforms appropriate for the Middle East. Looking out from the balcony of our transit hotel, one could see the golden sunlight on the tall towers of Nice and Cannes – a world of legendary glamour from which we were quickly to be flown away.

Little could I guess it at the time – the year was 1966 – that in later decades I would learn the slick trick of taking the helicopter from Nice into either Cannes or Monte Carlo – a very privileged way of breaking into these golden cities.

My first real acquaintance with Africa once again came by looking down from my aircraft window. Perfectly framed by the window was a large patch of brilliantly bright sand, with a camel towing a plough and the ploughman in desert djellaba, all of them casting razor sharp shadows on the sand, such as I had never seen in the UK.

⁘

VICTORY DAYS

I have a very distant memory of the day when the Allies invaded Normandy – announced to us in solemn tones on BBC Radio, broadcasting to us on an immensely advanced machine for its age. Clad in impressive walnut veneer, it placed a TV set on top of a radio with many dials, which in turn rested on a record player with a mechanism capable of dropping half a dozen discs in order. In this respect, my parents had been very advanced buyers of media. The TV set itself never played during the war.

33

But our teleradiogram – to coin a phrase – had a superb acoustic and in most of our houses it was our most important means of contact with the outside world.

I have no recollection of how the Tresilian family celebrated Victory in Europe (VE Day), but some seventy years on, I still remember with equal amounts of love and vividness my mother celebrating Victory in Japan (VJ Day) by using a ladder to climb a monkey puzzle tree and ornamenting it with flags.

❖

ANTHONY BURGESS AT THE CAFÉ ROYAL

The writer Anthony Burgess – known to his closer friends as John Burgess Wilson – lived in the Sussex village of Etchingham, near Kipling's house. He became a friend during my period as a trainee arts producer with Southern Television. When I moved from Southern Television to the BBC in London and a flat in Pimlico, we needed a new meeting place. John/Anthony suggested the Café Royal, and thereafter, we would meet when we could and drink from glasses still haunted by the spirits of Wilde, Whistler and other famous wits.

Though most famous nowadays for *A Clockwork Orange*, Burgess made his reputation with a trilogy of novels about life in contemporary Malaysia and a set of English-based novels featuring a grumpy anti-hero, Francis Xavier Enderby, a dyspeptic who wrote his poetry sitting on the loo and whose primary expletive was 'for cough'.

Burgess' wife, Lynne, always came too – she claimed she had obtained a better degree than her husband while at university and was visibly jealous of the fact that he had become famous and she not. She died before her husband, who then married an

Italian wife and started a new pattern of friendships.

Amongst my friends, he was remarkable for never learning to drive a car and always being able to find a taxi.

❖

WILLIAM GEAR

In my early days as a production trainee at Southern Television, I was put in touch with a supremely self-confident artist, who advertised himself as 'Britain's modern Michelangelo' and sold prints portraying faintly lubricious nude women – art for the bedroom wall. This big man had one ambition, which was to prove that abstract art was rubbish. This called for a confrontation.

At that time, the director of the Towner Gallery in Eastbourne was William Gear, an artist who had ended the war in Paris and who used his demob time to meet and talk with many of Paris' leading contemporary artists, including Atlan, da Silva, de Staël, Dubuffet, Hartung, Mathieu, Pignon, Poliakoff, Schoffer, Singier and Soulages – a generation largely dedicated to abstract art or its derivatives. Other English artists following the same path in Paris after the war were Eduardo Paolozzi, Alan Davie and William Turnbull. A date was fixed for a confrontation in Southern Television's studios.

The day arrived, and with it, Britain's modern Michelangelo, a big bristly man looking indeed quite ready to eat an abstract artist for breakfast. William Gear, on the other hand, was small and looked rather diffident. The presenter opened the show with an invitation to Britain's modern Michelangelo to demolish abstraction root and branch. Whether the novelty of the studio overcame him or whether what he contained was only bluster, Britain's modern Michelangelo fell silent and found nothing else to say. William Gear gave a perfect description of why the general public still in those days found abstract art a great difficulty and then went on to justify it as a way of looking at the world in terms of the simple and the random – the aesthetics of chaos as one might now say – and in the process opening a vast new territory of opportunities for visual artists. Britain's modern Michelangelo had nothing to add to that – the interview ended, like the old cartoon in *Punch* with a 'collapse of stout party'.

❖

MOLDOVAN WHO BROUGHT MILK TO MANHATTAN

Cruising down the Danube on one of the rows of benches on the top deck, I found myself sitting beside a small, sturdy man from Moldova. He kindly told me his story. He had taken the opportunity to emigrate from Moldova to Manhattan. There, glancing round for an entrepreneurial business opportunity, he saw that there was no regular supply of cows' milk to New York's busiest island. Therefore, he set up a dairy company to deliver milk wholesale on a daily basis to Manhattan, a business which was gratifyingly successful – whence he was now able to leave it all behind and sail down the Danube.

❖

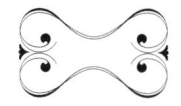

Malaga

ROOM 303

Every major city in Spain has its *parador* – a luxury hotel usually within the walls of some ancient mediaeval building, originally set up as part of a Utopian paradise planned by Franco, but still surviving long after his death, albeit the big chain of hotels is now in private hands.

The *parador* at Malaga was particularly pleasant to visit. It was high on a hill above the city, giving a view of one of Spain's most active mercantile ports. From the car park of the hotel, it is possible to look vertically downwards into the gaping circular mouth of the city's bullring. Experience taught me that not all the rooms facing the port and the Mediterranean beyond gave an untrammelled view – rows of pine trees had been erected in front of the hotel. We learned that the best room to book was named after the British rifle bullet which had sustained the army through two world wars – Room 303. It had a clear view between the pine trees and wonderful privacy.

EARLY MORNING ON MALAGA BEACH

It is good custom, when driving to Malaga Airport to pick up a visitor, to pause on the way and take a quick swim on Malaga beach before driving on to the turbulent melée of Malaga Airport. Particularly impressive on these early morning occasions was the solid queue of Malagan citizens of all shapes, ages and sizes walking with great determination along the sandy ridge of the beach, visibly fighting back death and celebrating the continuance of life. Had we decided to stay in Spain, Fay and I planned to move to a house in Malaga and join this death-defying population in their early morning walks. But our children lived too far away, and, in the end, Britain beckoned – albeit under the blanketing cultural foliage of the dreadful Brexit.

✣

PICASSO MUSEUM IN MALAGA

There is a fine museum of Picasso's works in Malaga, but it operates on a strange principle. One may go from gallery to gallery but only in one direction. Tall, strapping Andalucian girls police all the doorways to prevent you turning round and looking at a picture you had only just seen. It was frustrating for the art lover but somehow seemed to fit very neatly with the spirit of Spanish bureaucracy.

✣

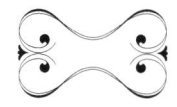

THE DRIVE ALONG BLUE RIDGE MOUNTAINS

An International Society for the Study of Time (ISST) council meeting was over; I had a hired car and had plenty of time to loiter in the USA before my flight home. I booked in for the night in a singularly featureless Hilton hotel. American hotels very often have no proper restaurant service – mine was no exception. I was directed to a restaurant half a mile away where I had an excellent dinner. Afterwards, I drove back to the Hilton but found myself confused by a choice of motorway exits and no sign for the presence of my hotel. I took the second exit – fortunately, someone bumped his horn to warn me. I was going up the wrong side of a two-lane freeway and roaring towards me, albeit still just at a safe distance, were a couple of gigantic American cargo vehicles. Fortunately, there was only a low kerb of bricks between me and the escape route on the other side. I jammed on my accelerator and skipped over the kerb to safety as the two vast vehicles whooshed by. I then quickly rediscovered the correct route to the hotel and slept like a soldier who had just escaped death. It was undoubtedly my most dangerous moment in the USA.

The next day, I found my way correctly onto the freeway. I noticed with interest that not one freeway junction was separated by a low kerb – all were separated by walls which I could never have crossed had I found myself in the predicament of the night before. A marginally wiser man, I drove on towards Gettysburg – a battle I had always wanted to know more about. The route lay across the Blue Ridge Mountains – a road hopping randomly between hilltops and valleys and full of winding corners. I came to the beginning of the ridge marked by a large road sign – but my expectations for a fun ride round sweeping bends in my slightly-tuned DeSoto car were squashed by a large notice setting a 35-mph speed limit. I drove with a certain cautiousness for the first couple of miles of the ridge but then was momentarily delayed by a mountainous crash of motorbikes. Already, police cars and ambulances were formed up and racing off with injured bodies to the nearest hospital behind me. I immediately realised that the motorcycle crash had created a useful distraction. All the traffic on the ridge would be rescue and emergency traffic, completely uninterested in whatever speed I was going. In effect, I had the ridge to myself. I jammed my foot on the accelerator and got the usual sigh of discontent from the big engine used to low revs, but gradually the power pulled through and soon I was flying along the ridge, driving fast corners like Fangio, and on my way completely unheeded to Gettysburg, while emergency vehicles raced past me in the opposite direction. It was an exhilarating drive.

Gettysburg is a most interesting battlefield to visit. It is best visited with the aid of a CD player to guide one around – easily obtained in local drugstores. American Civil War battlefields bear a unique psychological signature. The two armies of boys fought face to face in lines never far apart. It all feels intensely personal. My CD player took me around the battlefield on well-metalled roads, taking me through the sites of various famous skirmishes until finally, I reached the gateway to Pickett's Charge. This was where occurred the turning point of the battle and ultimately the turning point of the war. Here, General Robert E. Lee had thrown the weight of his infantry against the Unionist lines. The infantry marched in perfect order through the hayfields towards the stone wall, behind which the Union infantry lay spreadeagled and taking aim. Sadly, the hayfield was cluttered with large wooden racks for drying the hay. Federal troops who, in their impatience to cross the battlefield, tried to scale these wicked obstacles were shot down in their hundreds, only a residue reached the stone wall – it is still there

– to be massacred by their fellow countrymen on a face-to-face basis. General Robert E. Lee himself was said to have stood weeping at the gate of the field as the decimated residue of his troops staggered back to safety.

⁂

THE ENGLISH MASTER AND *GRAY'S ELEGY*

I went to an excellent prep school that sent lots of its boys on to compete for scholarships at top public schools. But some villain can always get through. The most extraordinary exponent of teaching I ever encountered was a cheerful fellow – straight from an Evelyn Waugh novel – who appeared in front of the sixth form as an English teacher one summer term. '*The curfew tolls the knell... the ploughman homeward plods his weary way...* Now take that second line: the ploughman homeward plods his weary way – and see how many times you can write the words in different order but retain the original scanning. For instance, homeward the weary ploughman plods his way... the homeward ploughman plods his weary way... I will be interested to see how you get on'. As I recall, he then sat at his desk and opened his copy of *The Sporting Times* until class was finished.

The following Wednesday and Saturday morning, he would turn up on time, ask politely whether the boys had had any new successes to talk of, and when a few variant lines had been reported, nodded his satisfaction and returned to his newspaper. How this educational buccaneer got away with it for a whole term, in an exceptionally well-run boarding school of a hundred boys and a dozen masters, is hard to say.

But in those days, so soon after World War II, Britain was afloat with individuals claiming various fake ranks and military characters for themselves.

PARKING ON ICE BESIDE A CHURCH IN CANADA

I had been lecturing in Newfoundland. Afterwards, Fay and I hired a car and began to drive north along the Newfoundland coast. Winter was approaching, and for the first time ever we saw and heard the grinding of packed sea ice against the beach. Presently, we came to a small fishing port with a typical New England chapel on a pier beside the harbour. We parked the car, went into the church and listened as the wind slapped furiously from the Atlantic Ocean. We admired the treen-like quality of the beautifully turned church furniture. We meditated on the lives of the English who had risked the vast journey across the Atlantic in their sailing boats to find freedom for their Puritan religion – which later would supply the moral drive for the economic growth of the America we came to know in the 20th century – a country which twice came decisively to our aid against Germany. But then, coming out of the church, I recognised that we had parked our car on a sheet of ice from which we would have to back out. We accomplished this tricky achievement, but to this day, I regularly think of that strong Atlantic wind taking our car by the side and pushing it into the harbour water, drowning us both. It was my second most dangerous moment in North America.

✥

MUSHROOM SOUP IN POLAND

In Poland, the beginning of spring is mushroom season. On the relevant day, the board of InfoRadio would suspend itself and go for a collective lunch at a local restaurant. Presently, waiters arrived with bowls of mushroom soup for us all. There would be a silence. Speechless glances were exchanged. Then everyone drank the potentially risky liquid. In my experience, no one ever died...

THERE BUT FOR THE GRACE...

We were staying with our friends the Alexanders in the Dordogne. The surrounding meadows were full of mushrooms. Fay and I came back from the nearest valley with a basket of attractive white mushrooms and emptied them onto the kitchen table to be trimmed for the salad. At that point there was a knock on the door and in came our mutual friend, Philippe Cousin, editor of the French scientific journal, *Science et Vie*. He took one look at the mushrooms on the kitchen table and turned pale. Reaching into a pocket, he brought out a cutting from the local newspaper. It described the death of an entire family caused by the eating of the nameless mushrooms we had just picked. We threw away all our mushrooms and proceeded to our hearty lunch. On the scale of near-death events, at least for exploding a broken hand grenade, the army had provided a bag of explosive fuse and detonators. There was no precautionary bag on that day in the Dordogne. It was arguably another close brush with death.

✣

CHELSEA NICK

I was once interrogated by the police. They summoned me to Chelsea Nick and a constable sat me down in an interrogation room with a tape recorder running. Apparently, someone had reported me getting into my car – actually a minivan – pulling out suddenly from the side of the road, hitting a passing car, doing serious damage and driving off without reporting myself to the police. The interrogation was very long and very iterative. It took me the better part of an hour to persuade the interrogating officer to step out of the police station and inspect the small scratch on my car, which had indeed occurred as I had pulled away from the kerb the night before. We agreed there was no grounds there for a case – even in the 1970s – and I went on my way. But whenever I hear of a police interrogation in the news, I remember the strange claustrophobic feeling of my hour with the interrogating officer in Chelsea Nick.

⁓

SIR HENRY PARKER BOWLES

Long after my grandfather, Frederick, died, my grandmother, Edith, (known as Gum-Gum) lived on as a widow at White Lodge in Silver Street, Enfield. White Lodge was the second grandest house in Enfield. Much the grandest was Forty Hall, a fine mansion with sweeping gardens, long since appropriated by the local Town Council, but in those days, the property of Sir Henry Parker Bowles. My grandmother and he were secretly in love and, indeed, were confidently rumoured to have travelled alone in a slam-door railway carriage all the way from Central London to Enfield – a risky setting for a grand romance. Some while later, the then Lady Parker Bowles died and my grandmother, in her widowhood, was deemed to be deeply disappointed that the invitation to a marriage that would make her mistress of Forty Hall was never offered. Whether their close relationship continued after the delivery of that snub, family legend does not record – but my grandmother never married again and died many years later with a pleasant Mills & Boon book in her hand.

⁓

A ROMANTIC TALE

It is a little-known fact that from 1918–1920 British armed forces were actively engaged in support of the Russian White Army – the residue of loyalists to the monarchy eventually snuffed out by the Bolsheviks' Red Army, generalled by Trotsky – himself later assassinated on the orders of Stalin.

During my father's later years, he and my mother were visited by an ancient warrior of that forgotten period – his military rank I forget, but his name was Rod Banks and his manner I remember as old-fashioned and charming. He always arrived with a large box of Charbonnel et Walker chocolates – the best in Britain. They were very expensive and a colossal luxury. After my father died, he continued to bring his annual gift to my mother, and with it, stories of the escape from Sebastopol by a Royal Naval destroyer – which was how the UK got its troops out of this now long-forgotten war. We only know that he died because the visits eventually stopped and the chocolates never again came, vanishing unannounced from one's friend's memory.

✣

VIVAT IMPERIUM

On the round-the-world trip for my client Reuters, I had the honour of an introduction to the Foreign Secretary of Kenya. We met in his office. I could not help noticing that the Philips map of the world with its many areas of pink, which had hung in the geography master's room at my prep school, also hung on the Foreign Secretary's wall. Kenya itself was still a pink space on the map, though the country had long been decolonised.

It was always my habit to go for a walk outside my hotel after dinner. After dinner in Nairobi, I had walked barely a couple of hundred yards when I was stopped by a group of four or five boys asking me for money. I had prudently gone out without a penny in my pocket and told them so but promised them I would have £100 for them the following evening at about the same time. The following evening, they jumped out of the forest at the right place and at the right time. I gave the tallest one the cash, we exchanged a few genuine pleasantries, and despite my obvious vulnerability, I was allowed to go on my way back to the hotel unharmed. It was my own very small contribution to the decolonisation of Kenya. They were very nice, bright kids.

⁌

TENOR WHO SANG FLAT

"That was very good," said my father-in-law, Edmund Compton, rising from his seat for the Glyndebourne interval, "except that the tenor sang flat."

"Oh no he didn't!" said a woman rising to her full height in the row in front of us. "I'm his wife and he sang perfectly in tune."

That was also the night that Mrs Thatcher came to the opera, looking very attractive in a thoroughly feminine way – no wonder she kept all those middle-aged politicians in tow.

⁌

EHEU! BBC TELEVISION CENTRE

I miss the BBC Television Centre. It was the most extraordinary building. If you knew your way around, you could surf the various Control Rooms and look down through the plate glass windows into the recording going on below. I particularly enjoyed watching *Z Cars*, a police thriller which was live every night. The Ford cars the policemen rode around in each had a projection screen immediately behind their rear windows to indicate the view from the driver's mirror. As a result, the studio floor was hazardous with trailing wires. So far as I know, none of the great list of *Z Cars* stars ever fell over them – to name Stratford Johns, Frank Windsor, James Ellis, Brian Blessed and many more names who found early stardom there.

Television Centre was a nest of hidden surprises. Propped up groggily against the East Tower whenever not in use, was Dr Who's big blue telephone box. In an office nearby were the BBC Armourers – a couple of ex-RAOC warrant officers keeping guard over a diverse army of pistols, rifles, machine guns and spooky objects firing strange projectiles.

The Television Centre was a drum: four circular floors surrounding a central fountain. The fountain had to be closed down because its insistent watery note sent too many people on journeys to the BBC loos. The circular corridors were interrupted at regular intervals by sets of swinging fire doors. The distance between the doors was nicely calculated so that, walking alone, one was in a constant state of anxiety as to whether to hold the door open for the person coming behind, or – after taking a view of their distance away – to gently let it slam in their face. The niceties and naughtiness of British social life were thus simultaneously integrated into the structure of the TV Centre.

❖

THE LONELY DONKEY ON THE BEAUFORT ESTATE

There was a wonderful field of wildflowers on a farm at Luckington owned by the Beaufort family. At the far end of this glorious field lived a very solitary donkey. When my neighbour's wife died – she and he had met in the Land Army – he was clearly lonely too, because on most afternoons he would drive his old van past my office window and down to the street called Cherry Orchard on the Beaufort estate, which possessed a gate through which the donkey could be observed as it chewed away at its floral paradise. I think the sight of the donkey helped cure the old man's loneliness. It must be admitted that his wife was much prettier!

✥

JACK BISHOP

Jack Bishop, at a certain age, was our builder in Luckington. Before the war, when unemployment was really pinching on account of the great recession, Jack would bicycle daily some thirty miles to work on an immense new air base being built for RAF personnel and stores. At the end of every day, come hell or high water, he would remount his bike and plod the thirty miles home to tea in Sherston. A working day unthinkable in our times.

✥

A HELICOPTER ASSAULT

In the early 1980s, HMS Hermes, the slant deck aircraft carrier was harboured in Hong Kong. In 1898, Britain had obtained a 99-year lease on Hong Kong as part of the settlement of the Opium Wars. In 1997, the lease would be up, and Britain would be under obligation to deliver Hong Kong to its original masters, the Chinese. By the 1980s, the lease was nearly up. To emphasise the point, a group of Chinese Communist activists occupied one of Hong Kong's many financial tower buildings. At that time, British military power was represented by the aircraft carrier Hermes, converted into a helicopter carrier and heavily populated with Marines.

The Squadron Leader at that time was my intrepid cousin, Commander Rae Duxbury RN. Rae received orders to land a company of Marines on the occupied building and thereby take it over again for the British crown. A rehearsal would have been convenient – but it would have given the game away. So, it became my cousin's duty to calculate the velocity and angle of approach which would bring his Wessex helicopters, fully laden with Marines, to a soft landing on the roof of the tall building. Armed only with this calculation on paper, my cousin Rae briefed his squadron of helicopter commanders, brought the Wessex aircraft quickly on to deck and ordered them to fly flat out to the base of the occupied building, and over the last couple of hundred yards, flew back the controls and fly vertically to the top of the tower, there to disembark their crews.

The operation was brilliantly successful. The Chinese activists were deeply demoralised by the sight of the stomachs of the Wessex helicopters flying vertically to the summit of the building. Each helicopter hovered over the top of the building to discharge its Marines in full fighting order and then flew on to make room for the next attacker. Faced with a company of fully-armed and determined Marines, the Chinese activists were quick to surrender, and the event was over.

But I have wondered ever since why it was that my cousin Rae who led the hazardous assault was never awarded a military decoration. Perhaps HM Government – in the form of the Rt Hon. Christopher Patten, our last Governor of Hong Kong – did not want to advertise the event. There's no doubt in my mind, however, that the unrehearsed attack carried out at night in Hermes' squadron of ancient Wessex helicopters and guided only by my cousin's pencil and paper calculations was an act of considerable dash, even reckless courage – I am happy there were no casualties.

✥

THROWN OUT OF THE HOTEL

The war was not yet over but the mines had been cleared from East Anglia's beaches, and my parents decided to take my sister and myself for our first seaside holiday. The Sandilands Hotel in the vicinity of Skegness was identified as a suitable resort – indeed, I still remember the Tunnel of Love on the *papier-mâché* mountain with a stream running through it, along which the visitor travelled in a dinghy gripped by an underwater cable, to watch various exotic scenes such as a Red Indian village – a phrase possible then but no longer now – and a sugar plantation. My sister Liz and I were duly impressed by this outpouring of fantasy after all the years of war – it was a great disappointment, when I returned to Skegness some twenty years later, to find that the Tunnel of Love had disappeared.

Our base for these adventures was, as I have said, the Sandilands Hotel. But this was a hotel that took no prisoners and, when my father complained about being given pre-sweetened Camp coffee for his breakfast, the entire Tresilian family was thrown out. The local signal master must have been used to this kind of fracas generated by Sandilands because he very kindly put us up for the rest of our stay. My memory still retains an image of hard grey waves slamming up against the dunes which protected the low-lying area around Skegness.

Many years later, I was driving with my wife Fay on a return journey from the north of England, where we had gone to escape the burning heat of summer 1976. Suddenly I saw a sign for the Sandilands Hotel. We parked in the car park and were immediately greeted by the first of the many instructions - printed by the management and exhibited on card - to keep the guests in order. 'No children in the dining room after 6pm'. 'No informal dress beyond this point' and so on – there were cards with instructions on them wherever one could shift one's eyes. Clearly, across the years the hotel had not changed its strict disciplinary approach to customers. It was a curiously reassuring message from the past that the value systems of a certain class of English hotel still fiercely survived.

Looking at the AA map of the region, Sandilands Hotel no longer seems to be trading.

✥

CORIN REDGRAVE'S CALFSKIN TROUSERS

A special relationship existed between the Marlowe Society in Cambridge – dedicated to Shakespearean drama – and the Royal Shakespeare Company at its home in Stratford-upon-Avon. Peter Hall's brilliant spell as a director at Cambridge had endowed the Marlowe Theatre Company with special gravitas. It was manifest during my time at Cambridge when Corin Redgrave – the hyper-intelligent son of Sir Michael Redgrave

– father of an entire dynasty of young theatrical Redgraves, agreed with John Barton, *dramaturg* of the Royal Shakespeare Company at Stratford, to use the Marlowe Company to do a trial dry run of Shakespeare's Henry VI, parts I, II and III – an epic in early Shakespearean historical verse, with the prospect of this largely forgotten megadrama being revived at Stratford if the performance at the Marlowe turned out successful.

Corin Redgrave, it turned out, had an extraordinary stage-memory. As he blocked the play, scene by scene – that is to say, gave the actors their moves – the normal theatrical director would expect to be supported by an assistant who would record the moves in a book. Corin needed no such assistant. Every move, as blocked, would take an indelible place in his memory – even errors in the movements of marginal actors like myself would be observed and picked on. Stratford gave its assistance, too. The set for this hugely complex historical play was exceedingly plain: a series of brownish drapes surrounding the acting area, onto which lights were projected. I once spent an entire afternoon listening to the Stratford theatre lighting expert bringing the drab stage-space to life with orders to lights I couldn't see and with results too finely nuanced for my eyes to register. Corin, I may add, kept order on stage partly by the Rolls Royce efficiency of his brain, but partly also by wearing a pair of brown calfskin trousers which were a talking point amongst women whenever Corin had just passed by.

These were the days when the upper middle classes veered instinctively to the Left in their political thinking. Corin and his sister Vanessa, identifying themselves as Trotskyists, co-founded the Workers' Revolutionary Party – in its wide-ranging eclecticism and vagueness of purpose, a sort of political equivalent of the Anglican church.

❖

THREE OF CLUBS

It is a matter of some shame to most respectable Spaniards that the entire country is laced with brothels – usually known as *'clubs'*. La Carlota had a brothel at each end of the town. *S'candalo* (pronounced without the 's') was beside a motorway garage and had a big car park for lorries. The 'Club' at the far end of the town was in those days noted for its Ukrainian girls. Most curious of all was the *Luna Club*, whose slogan was *'solo pareja'* – which translated into English means 'partners only'. In other words, couples were expected to go in two by two, like species on the Ark – the Spanish equivalent of 'wife-swapping' parties said to be popular in the Home Counties of the UK. Like other Las Pinedas businesses, the *Luna Club* was situated in the main industrial estate. There were many old couples in Las Pinedas. History does not record what the *Luna Club* meant for them...

❖

YOU'VE NEVER HAD IT SO GOOD

I will never forget Harold Macmillan emerging from the Rose and Crown Inn in Chipping Sodbury, half pint silver mug in his hand, to toast the town and tell its citizens – these were literally his words – "You've never had it so good."

❖

A LUMP IN MY THROAT

Halfway through Cambridge, I became increasingly worried by a lump in my throat. Finally, I took myself to the Addenbrooke's Hospital and found a friendly consultant in A&E. He told me to open my mouth, took a look inside and said: 'Have you been acting recently?' I had indeed been acting recently – the consultant told me I was straining my voice, and my period of panic was over.

❖

LADIES' NIGHT IN OLDHAM

No man with a healthy desire for personal survival will wander the streets of Oldham on a Thursday night. Thursday night in Oldham is Ladies' Night. Gangs of yelling women patrol the streets and flow into the pubs – I was in Oldham on a Thursday night and remember those sounds well. All wise men in Oldham stay at home on Thursday night. In this city of many mills, the men were paid on Friday and then went to the pub.

❖

A QUESTION TO THE ORACLE

One of my great delights when the family was on holiday was to remove one of the children for a couple of days of private life. When the family was on holiday in Crete, my mother included, sunbathing in the most modern way, I took Arabella with me on a boat to Piraeus – the port which is also the gateway to Athens itself. She was in her teens and open to every kind of classical experience. We took rooms in a hotel on Syntagma Square. The square is the very heart of commercial activity and Greek politics. Its name – which literally means 'the arrangement' – commemorates an agreement forced on King Otto, the first king of Greece, in 1843, by a popular military uprising. We spent the evening in an excellent restaurant watching the European Cup Final on TV, in which Liverpool in their prime destroyed Real Madrid.

The next morning, we rose early to get into the Acropolis before the crowds arrived. They quickly came, winding up the hill in great sluglike charabancs with blackened windows. We managed a thorough visit of this extraordinary space before the crowds of tourists packed it too densely to be enjoyed.

Our next voyage of adventure was to Mycenae. There again, the black slug charabancs were advancing in a ceaseless queue up the hill to a car park more or less masking the city. But the real mystery here lay underground. Mycenae possesses two 'beehive' tombs, deeply dug with a ground level entrance, an internal shape modelled on a traditional straw beehive but greatly expanded – coming to a point far above the floor. This configuration defined a natural centrepoint on the floorplan where I went to stand. I spoke to Arabella, but she couldn't hear me. However, what I heard was my own voice producing a vast echoing, godlike sound which must have been known to the makers of the tomb and which, surprisingly, I have never seen mentioned in literature on Mycenae. (I should add that a similar vast magnification of a simple voice can be heard within the entrance hall of the Central School of Art and Design on Southampton Row!) I still hear that immense, inaudible sound that my daughter could not hear from outside the sound column, yet which I heard as though I were Zeus himself giving orders to the more mischievous lesser gods.

Later, to have another experience of mystic voices from the past, we drove to Delphi which, as well as containing a horse-racing track, conceals the deep and mysterious cave of the Oracle. The Oracle was well known for speaking in riddles which required decoding by priests, but there was no voice of the Oracle on that particular afternoon and a distinct absence of priests. As for the racetrack, positioned so close to the Oracle, we were left uninformed but able to reflect philosophically on the relationship between risk that could be raced for and overtly won and risks which rested on riddles whose solution might only be disclosed by disaster.

Astonishingly, the Pierian spring emerged from a metal pipe on the edge of the road. I made sure Arabella drank of this nectar which had so effectively inspired the poets of Greece – the water was free, but it has proved a good investment. Arabella may not classify formally as a poet, but she is a great worker with words.

⁜

JANE RUSSELL

Jane Russell was one of those Hollywood stars whose legs were said to be insured for a million dollars. Full length photos of her in the costumes of various films hung on every cabin wall in the US Navy during the war against Japan. When an actor is so famous, one is disinclined to consider their later years. But even great stars must earn money to stay alive. In the 1970s – long after the height of the Russell fame – there was a large cabaret club on the Mendip Hills, south of Bristol, where she had come to perform. I interviewed her there for regional television. Once one of the most famous women in the world, her manner now was modest and friendly. The famous sabre-cutting legs were hidden from view in a pair of navy-blue slacks. She was deglamourised but as much of a trooper as ever. She would sing and dance in some dramatic costume of sequins and silk, and go on her way around the world. With the war now long over, how many of the club's big Bristol audience would have known remotely who she was and why her fame, in those years of fast-fading memories, could only be guessed at.

✥

THE ROMAN CENTURION

Outside the mediaeval village of Castle Combe is an ancient bridge of flat stones crossing the Bybrook – this being the name of the river that waters the valley. One day, a husband and wife came into my mother's antique shop in a state of high excitement, asking, "Is there any name for that bridge just along the river?"

My mother replied offhandedly, "It's always been called the Roman Bridge."

Both husband and wife turned marginally apoplectic. Moments ago, they had been standing on the bridge when they were aware of a third party standing beside them: a sturdy man dressed entirely in a leather costume – by all appearances a Roman Centurion. They left the bridge hurriedly, partly out of fear, partly to convey their news.

Another friend, to whom I introduced the bridge, began speaking of Saxons in woven costumes performing some ritualistic sacrifices.

One is never entirely alone in the British countryside. The spirits are always active.

✥

BREAKFAST WITH THE BABUSHKAS IN ST PETERSBURG

Our journey down the Neva River had been held up by ice and snow, and our cruise boat had not yet arrived. We were put in buses with grinding wheels and propelled to a deeply depressing hotel where somehow, we survived the night. The next morning, we followed the signs to breakfast to find a restaurant unstaffed and completely without signs of food. With due English fortitude, the entire company set off to a neighbouring restaurant, also unstaffed, but well-equipped with bread and the usual accessories. We helped ourselves and carried our triumphal goods back to our own restaurant. Before we had the chance to sit down and make ourselves comfortable, an angry flotilla of hotel babushkas ran into our dining room and removed all our stolen booty. I still remember these misshapen middle-aged ladies disappearing from our dining-room with slices of bread between their fingers. I believe – and hope – that we somehow in the end obtained fresh bread and later that day, our cruise liner appeared and, bar the usual obligatory visit to a large gift shop relating commercially to the hotel, we finally found ourselves on our Soviet cruise liner nosing out into a bay full of small icebergs – the point of entry of the River Neva into the Russian continent.

❖

BETRAYED BY A BOTTLE OF RUM

There is a solitary hill – a glacial remainder – which projects sharply from the grassy plains of Cheshire. It is known in military circles as the Bickerton Feature. Nights spent in muddy trenches and days spent crawling on one's stomach between tussocks of heather were the climax to our battle training. No one who has spent a night in mud under an army blanket will ever forget the fearful stench these covers emit. However, I had secured some comfort. In my upper left-hand pocket, I had secreted a quarter bottle of rum with which to celebrate the end of our military adventures. As I crawled through rain-soaked tussocks and searched vainly for an 'enemy' no doubt as miserable as myself, the thought of the rum in my pocket gave me the encouragement I needed to survive this grisly ordeal. Finally, night manoeuvres came to an end and there in front of us, miraculously, was a fully lit marquee. I dived into the marquee, ignored the tea on offer and dived into my left-hand breast pocket for my longed-for bottle of rum. I unscrewed the lid, and the bottle was empty – its entire contents of rum had soaked away in the night. However, military life does not leave much time for lamentation. We now had to pick up our backpacks, pouches and rifles ready for the supreme test – the twenty-eight-mile march back to our battle camp headquarters at Eaton Hall. I have never really trusted rum again.

❖

BUYING LYPSYL IN BULGARIA

It was cold when I first arrived in Bulgaria. Sofia, the capital, lies amongst the foothills of a mountain, so I quickly had chapped lips. It is normal in England to reach out at the chemist and help oneself to a tube of Lypsyl. But try doing that in Bulgarian, a completely unknown language. Worse still, each time I stood in front of a pharmacist and signed the application of lipstick to my lips, the wrong impression was clearly received. I think I must have ended up with a bottle of Nivea cream. Some very strange looks followed me as I left the shop.

MY FATHER AND BANANAS

My father came back from war service in America with his head full of Freud. He had already closed his mind to the idea of bringing us up – my sister and myself – as American children protected by Freudian superstitions. But now, as it turned out, his return to England coincided with the arrival of the first shipment of bananas since the beginning of the war. My mother had acquired half a dozen and displayed them proudly on the luncheon table for my father's first meal on his return to England. But my beloved father had read about bananas in Freud and knew they were phallic symbols and, therefore, rather rude. I don't know how my mother persuaded him to overcome his anxieties about the banana.

Years later, however, I plucked up the courage to ask if my father had been gallant. "Very," announced my mother, with considerable conviction. It was not a question I needed to ask again.

❖

CLEARING THE BEDS FROM NETLEY HOSPITAL AFTER SUEZ

Netley Hospital was a vast Victorian structure dating from the time of the Crimean War, stretching along the sides of the Solent and, alas, demolished in the 1960s. At the time of the Suez venture, when Britain had been forced to withdraw by the American Foreign Secretary, Dulles, my entire platoon was taken off Basic Training and driven to Netley to remove the many hundreds of beds that had been stored there in advance of the Suez campaign. The Ministry of Defence had been preparing for many more casualties than the public ever imagined.

❖

DAVID NIVEN AS AN ARMY OFFICER

During World War II, the young David Niven starred in the film *The Way Ahead* (1944), in which he played a young subaltern from a rifle regiment conscripted, trained, and given the task of knocking into military order a platoon of his own reluctant countrymen. The film ended with the platoon going into attack in Italy. As Niven and his men advanced into the smoke and flames of their first battlefield, Niven threw away the pistol which would have identified him as an officer and took up the rifle of one of his platoon who had already fallen. It was a moment of surprising candour in an official military film. I made it my resolve to copy David Niven and disguise myself as an Other Rank if ever National Service took me into battle – which fortunately it never did.

❖

KYIV AND LVIV

When Russia crashed its forces into the beautiful cities of Ukraine in 2014, I had visited only recently before with our Bulgarian friends the Pountchev family who had a house in Kyiv, only a day's flight from the legendary spires of Lviv – also known as Lvov, and in Austrian imperial days as Lemberg, in the process re-igniting the familiar fears of a Cold War – so relatively recently abandoned by a Western world which had unwisely believed that liberal democracy had won the battle over state Communism.

As 2023 news bulletins repeatedly announce attacks by Russian drones and rockets on the electrical generators and fresh water of the major Ukrainian cities, my mind goes back to Kyiv and Lviv as I saw them in their brief period of peace: graceful cities with relaxed young people moving with the same freedom that we see amongst the young on European streets with their open cafés and restaurants.

✧

A FLASH OF AMERICAN GENIUS

In the great pooling of talents during World War II it fell to my father, then Chief Engineer of Armstrong Siddeley, who had just rectified two of their dysfunctional rotary engines, the Deerhound and the Wolfhound, to be seconded to the USA to work with American aircraft companies on a particular problem besetting them at that time: the tendency of their aircraft to crash. (Many years later in *All My Sons* Arthur Miller wrote a play on this very subject which my life-long friend Lawrence Gordon-Clark and I co-produced at the Arts Theatre in our final term at Cambridge in 1962). My father obtained much honour in the USA and when the war came to an end was offered various high-ranking positions in various US aircraft and motor car companies. But by then he had resolved that he and my mother could never be American-style parents to their children – fearful of trampling on their little Freudian egos etc – and so he returned to a rather less satisfactory engineering career in the UK, but where he and my mother could speak to their children frankly – that is to say, to my sister and myself.

During my father's time in the USA however he had acquired some very good American friends. One in particular, Major Ed

Hall (Edward Nathaniel Hall, 1914-2006) had been amongst many US personnel charged with evaluating German industrial and scientific achievements during the course of World War II.

Infinitely frustrated by the bureaucratic confusion and clutter which surrounded this activity, Major Hall submitted his own brilliantly imaginative spoof report on the supposed 'discovery' of German underground factories used apparently for constructing aircraft produced in 'lighter-than-air metal' - a material he called 'Balloonium'.

With its exquisite detailing – e.g. the reverse curvature on aircraft wings to prevent them from flying into outer space – Ed Hall's entirely-invented report stormed its way through layers of credulous bureaucrats and actually reached the Pentagon before his glorious deception was unmasked.

He then rewrote this, by now infamous, parody report as a letter (23.07.43) to my father and mother – Tres and Stew were both nicknames which my father had attracted during his US years.

I break my own rule of sole authorship in favour of Ed Hall, to share this short piece. It is truly a triumph of the American comic genius. I offer it in memory of all those American flyers who gave their lives over Europe in World War II.

23.7.1943

Dear Tres, Wife, Progeny and All,

It's really too bad you missed out on this deal, Stew. In absolute compliance with policies and directives of the USAAF dealing with the employment of no engineers in engineering, no cooks in cooking, etc., no-one possessing traces of intelligence had been employed in the organisation. It was a hell of a good idea; I'm all for it, judge for yourself.

One of the first and most important projects we've handled, "Project Important" had to do with the location and acquisition of balloonists from German sources. This material, as you doubtless know, possesses a specific gravity lower than that of air, and a strength somewhat in excess of 24 ST. As a number one on the list of strategic materials required by Uncle Sam for prosecuting the war against the Japs, this material was sought avidly. Preliminary surveys revealed a fair-sized mountain of balloonite, the ore from which balloonium is refined, at a secret location in Germany. Since in the past, supplies of this material have been strictly limited (so much so in fact, that use of the stuff was strictly prescribed except for the correction of errors of airplane designers on the West Coast – naturally automatically assigning it all to Consolidated), this find created a major sensation. A large party was despatched immediately to ship some of the junk to Air Technical Service Command, Right Field. This proved a complete flop. As the kids dragged hunks of ore from the shaft mouth (rolling it along the ceiling, naturally), it took off. In these instances where smaller masses were loaded on trucks, the roofs failed and when the roofs were reinforced, the trucks lacked sufficient traction for the trip back. Oh! My aching back! In one section where several sections of fabricated balloonium shapes were unearthed (stacked down instead of up) the kid dragging out the lowest piece was seriously injured when it struck him on the chin and charged into the roof. We are now equipping a unit to properly handle these activities – lead soled shoes for personnel, ballast and reinforced roofs in trucks, and a C.47 with wings mounted upside down for long hauls.

While these frenzied activities were taking place, another series of game genii were intensively attacking the problem of best disposition of this vital material with marked success. They finally came up with the following proposition. A specification was to be drawn up at A.T.S.C. W.F.O. for the manufacture of a flying wing. It was further to be specified that this machine was to be built of balloonium. Now, a wing is affixed to an airplane for the sole purpose of providing lift. Since this gadget was to be fabricated of balloonium, it did not need lift, hence it did not require wings. But the machine was to be a flying wing – only wings – therefore, it did not have to be built at all. Merely laying down the specification properly would immediately equip the country, with no great economic dislocation involved, with a huge force of these machines.

One difficulty then became apparent – how to find the damn things afterwards. One could grope around a hangar filled with these marvellous machines for hours and find nothing. Fortunately, a solution to this small problem appeared at just the right moment. Word reached the office that a Czech monster had been located who could paint airplanes so that they were rendered invisible. Instructions had been immediately sent out to have this monster pickled (corrosion treated), crated for overseas shipment, and sent to A.T.S.C. W.F.O. God, what does not go to A.T.S.C. W.F.O!

We immediately countermanded the instructions and ordered the monster to be brought into the office (everything else is, from rocket fuel to jet engines). We figured that it should be a very simple trick for such a talented gent to reverse his process and paint something that isn't there so that it is visible.

While awaiting the arrival of this unique individual, Col. Al Deyarmond (he's a hell of a good guy, by the way) and I were discussing the above at lunch one day. A Major from our Intelligence Section was sucking it all in. Al finally gave the poop on the whole thing while I tried hard not to squirt out a mouthful of coffee all over the room. He finally advised the Major to notify the State Dept. thru the American Embassy in Paris of this important find.

Poor little man – he did. Now he's in a replacement depot.

This literary masterpiece so far relates only to one of our saner minor projects. This could continue for hundreds of pages, but I've no intention of making a martyr of you or wasting that much ink. Suffice it to be known that we've been mixed up in hauling elephants (real ones with trunks) out of Krautland by G.I. truck; interviewing 'top ranking Germans engineering personnel' who usually turned out to be janitors (the Germans following our own practice call these characters 'Chief Engineers' and our great men are always properly impressed); conducting a party of Kraut engineers and families ranging from 2 to 60 years old across most of Germany – this was particularly interesting since we spoke no German and they no English.

My job, incidentally, has been to investigate German jet and rocket work – I was picked no doubt, because of never having been cleared for this stuff or 'stoff' as our Heinies would say. It's really been most interesting technically, even though that place has been run purely as an adjunct to the gigantic scrap metal drive called Tech Intelligence Work. Though the Germans were not really very far advanced in the overall picture, they put up a good show for the P.N.O. (Public Relations Officer in U.S. Army – Propaganda in ours) by using equipment which we would consider in the development stage – a good way to lose a war. I did finally find out why we won – we were dumb; the Germans inconceivably thick. Back to the engineering picture, they did have some very cute techniques in detail design and manufacturing methods which I'd like to mull over with you sometime. Some would be most interesting I'm sure. We should be back in Merrie Olde within a month – buzz you then.

Be good
Ed.

Major Ed Hall
23rd July 1943

✥

FLEETS FLYING HOME

I was six years old when the invasion was announced on the radio. In Weybridge where we then lived, it turned into one of those lyrical long English summers with blue skies every evening. And every evening across the blue sky flew the returning bomber fleet of the US Air Force after day-bombing somewhere over Europe (the specialty of the American bomber force). The returning flights, many hundreds of planes at a time, droned home in the same perfect formation they had adopted on the way out to defend themselves against the hordes of German fighters which, still at that time in the war, flew up to intercept them. Invariably, despite their heavy defensive armaments, not all these Flying Fortresses and Liberators survived the day. Even as a six year old I could understand those hard facts by the gaps which intermittently appeared in the otherwise perfect geometric formation of the immense air fleet returning home to its bases in northern and east England. It's hard to imagine now but it's also something you never forget.

✥

CESARE THE CAT

Our neighbours – she, Teresa, an Italian journalist reporting on England; he, Pavel, a well known scientist in the field of lasers and nanoparticles – had acquired a dog to live in their house. It was a busy, noisy, barky dog and greatly offended the chief cat of the family, a beautiful marmalade pin-up of a cat by name of Cesare. Cesare took a look around the local village and saw that we Tresilians had no cat. He appointed himself our cat and without further notice became a fixture in our house, perched on chairs or lounging on sofas and at night lying on top of the blankets so that I could periodically tickle the top of his luxuriantly haired head.

Eventually the moment of truth arrived when Teresa entered our house for a cup of coffee and there was Cesare winking at her like a well-mannered host, but clearly intending to stay on in our house. Only Teresa's sons were upset by this.

It was the period of lockdown for COVID and our Cumnor house had the good fortune of a long lawn, up and down which I would march vigorously while being read to the novels of Trollope on my telephone by Audible. For a while the cat watched me, then it decided to join in, and from then on each time I walked the lawn he would trot up behind me, turn sharply at the far end and trot back again behind me. We made a rare and wonderful team. I was very touched that this Italian-speaking cat should be so fond of me.

✢

Printed in Great Britain
by Amazon